Driving Face Down

Driving Face Down

Poems by
Doren Robbins

LYNX HOUSE PRESS
SPOKANE, WASHINGTON/PORTLAND, OREGON

Cover art by James Lowrey
Cover design by Scott Poole
Page design by Joelean Copeland

Acknowledgments
Grateful acknowledgments to the editors and publishers of the journals and
chapbooks in which the following poems appeared, sometimes in an earlier
version.

Brass City: "The Red Fan"
Electric Rexroth: "Driving Face Down"
Five A.M.: "Gregor Samsa's Face"
Genre: "Chaos With Waterfowl"
Hayden's Ferry Review: "Beneath The Jewish Music"
Kiosk: "My Pico Boulevard"
Shirim: "Jewdog" and "Abrams"
Spillway: "Mask"
Sulfur: "The Injury In My Mouth Tells Me,"
Willow Springs: "Marc Chagall and the Male"

Library of Congress Cataloging-in-Publication Data

Robbins, Doren.
        Driving face down: poems / by Doren Robbins
                p. cm.
        ISBN 0-89924-109-3 (alk. paper)
                I. Title.

PS3568.O229 D75 2001

                                                    2001029446

"My Pico Boulevard," "Anna," "Driving Face Down," "Gregor Samsa's Face," "The Injury in my Mouth Tells Me," "Jewdog," and "The Red Fan" appeared in the chapbook *Dignity In Naples And North Hollywood* (Pennywhistle Press,1996. Introduction by Philip Levine). "Marc Chagall and the Male Soul" appeared in the chapbook *Under The Black Moth's Wings* (Ameroot Press, 1988). "Beneath the Jewish Music" appeared in the pamphlet *Onionman* (Rabble-A Press, 1998). "Clinic" was a commendation prize winner awarded from The Chester H. Jones Foundation, and appeared in their annual anthology in 1996. "Jewdog," " 'The Sailor,'" and "Beneath the Jewish Music," won first prize for the Anna Davidson Rosenberg Award given by the Judah Magnes Museum 1996.

I would also like to thank Oregon Literary Arts and The Centrum Residency Program for fellowships which allowed me to complete this book.

Lynx House Press books are distributed by
Small Press Distribution, 1341 Seventh Street, Berkeley, CA 94702
Lynx House Press
420 W. 24th Ave.
Spokane, WA 99203
and
9305 SE Salmon Ct.
Portland, OR 97216

Sincere gratitude and thanks to Linda Janakos, Dorianne Laux, and Philip Levine for their clear insights about improving as well as arranging some of the poems in this book. And to Sharon Doubiago, Bill Mohr, and Gerald Stern for their support and encouragement. And to Michael C. Ford for all the Jazz.

Contents

PART ONE

TWINE TIME

Always the camellias break first.
And I get forced in, I get caught
in the shower of them, and the hotter one
within my wrist. In wood powder I rode
into camellias, stopping my cut on the stringer
for the new stairs . . . the usual irregular attention,
leaning down gathering cut wood,
blurred in the spray of saw dust,
the funeral of a beak down there,
the ants jagged at the slab edge
along the plywood siding . . . and I crouch
beside camellias, facing the wall
of my twine—the camellias break
while I saw on the ground they root
in a shower from. And I want,
as I always do, a road
coming out of them,
and raspberry briars
if they have to come with it—
something floral I always want
to be extended from—and I need a table there
with a bowl on it, and maybe not a road yet
with camellias raised by a wall—
I never completely depend on a road—
but that table with a bowl of my fruit,
and with starlings coming over the raspberry needles,
a table with a bowl of pears I reach for
for their sweetness, admiring the ones
with leaves that come unbroken with the stems,
and for the skin that lasted, and the core
I leave for the squirrels and the woodchucks,
and the syrup I leave for the hornets and the ants,

the limes tight in the shade behind them—pears,
and the storm they come out of
in their yellow leather, with ripened spots
and unripened spots still part of eachother—
even when it means coming up against the usual wall
of twine to reach them, even when it means
I get forced into my own storm—
another sweating day, another last
of the straws—I'll take the fat layers
that come with it, and the twine layers,
always the barren with the sweet, together—
I'll take the weak skin it is composed of
as much as anything, I'll take my tools
back in with me one way or the other,
I'll take the song the saw teeth make,
and I'll take the camellias
breaking their melons on my eyes, I'll take the herb
their shadows secrete, I'll take the floral
when I can get it, I'll take it without a road.

Ma's Ma

After she stopped calling her own children because she knew
no one could bear her cynical crying and all of her organs
were bitter and she shook her head at her useless ankles and tore off
a piece for me from a braided horn of pastry, I didn't
say a thing, just looked at the rough edges

of the big hand she chopped calf liver and chicken skin with, the cleaver
a loud clicking toy in her grip. Then one of the big arms got caught-up
       in her robe and she turned it through the sleeve finally
and distinguished with her fingers

the candies and bus-transfers, make-up and coupons unused for
months and worried, and looked for, and didn't find
       a great-grandchild's gift—
complaining the whole time about the smell in her purse—
worrying about the lost thing, a wrapper, a pencil
with lead broken-off,

weeping with neurotic vulnerability about the smell—
then took my hand, giving that look, shaking her head
from side to side, delighted beyond what I perceived
watching her tilt and raise her face in that manner,

rising on her toes aged into rough thorns
coming through one slipper, shifting her eyes
over my eyes, tilting her head, grabbing my face
in her hands, kidding me, saying, "How *homely* you are,
who will ever marry you!?"

"The Sailor"

She didn't understand a thing why he left for the ruins
in Greece, or the Yucatan, and began to call him "the sailor."
Didn't refer to him as "the sailor"

out of endearment, either, but as an attack—
because she knew a sailor was swept by a weather
that sent a man away from the world or back to it

beyond a shore she could recognize.
Neither did she understand why "the sailor" didn't marry
the woman he lived with, or why he lived alone,

or when he decided to finally marry why he didn't talk
about adding to her 17 great-grand-children—
and why did he always sweat when he talked,

why did he eat excessively without regard,
or why was he unashamed to go from job to job
saying the "opportunities" were unforgivable,

and why did he want to be "a sailor" in the first place?
how could he envy the hardened ones who endured only
on the floor of cold seas? Why envy Gogol or Dostoyevsky?

"Flies in the milk your Gogol and Dostoyevsky, I don't like
flies in the milk—why drink it, that milk with flies in it?"
And why did he insult all her celebrities for their politics while

the family celebrated at weddings and births—why did he
have to believe with Tacitus "that even when it fails
wickedness finds followers"—and what was it with him

that he thought the crew in the kitchen where he worked, and the uncles
who worked as tailors or salesmen, and the neighbors who left 2 hours
before opening so they could make it on time to jobs
at Northrop Aircraft, or Standard Oil, were trapped

like he and all the rest in that neighborhood were trapped—
producing weapons, and clothing, weapons, meals, oil
and weapons and why didn't he

shield her from all this?

THE INJURY IN MY MOUTH TELLS ME

Today even standing in a cut rag, Mrs. Penser, in 5th Street Market,
and all the nose and eyelid rings—today people at 5th Street
enchant me their way, parade their pain, their holes

down to me worthwhile in rings, in skin, in a coat
ripped down the back. Even the injury in my mouth
tells me to look, points out what to listen for, as though listening

had not yet been enough, and I never really saw what putting
holes into yourself, or getting holes, could be about.
We are full of holes, no matter what Mrs. Penser will not say,
no matter her deformed fingers,

no matter which Gestapo jail guard creaming his pants twisting pliers
on her hand and will never be found. Even the smell of your dogs
            on you today

or the canary that used to sleep on your pillow and dirty it
for your care—also a pleasure dear to you—

even standing as you rock while stroking

your Spatzie, adorable white-pawed stray dog, your own eyes
closed, Mrs. Penser. No matter what holds my upper body hair to me,
I stir coffee with an arm clogged into holes, the green formica
my elbows row into the granules of, plywoods of poison adhesives

delaminated in one ruffled corner where a layer parted its lid
so the dust of the glue could enter me. No matter what smoke
blown chain-smoked into blue numbers, no matter whose wrist
made part blue, etched blue, it was all holes when I looked.
No matter what, I let her graze her cold hole into me,
all her stumps,

three yellowed crushed nails row on my hair and my hair
sucks onto them, glad for nose and eye lid rings, glad
her death camp fingers are unshawled by gloves—
glad for nipple, glad for foreskin, glad for labial hoops.
Glad the dishonesty didn't work, glad the relatives prohibiting
the urge to look, glad their trying to contain the impulse to shudder,
didn't work. And Mrs. Penser, bending down to nurse me in the dream,
her bra full of staples and roaches. No wince. No blame.

Glad I noticed my mother's stricken reassuring look,

picking up dishes through her long-haired hole, stroking Mrs. Penser's
knobby shoulder while she dexterously lit cigarettes
with her two regular fingers, in the room with the pools

of all their smoke. A room of stacked holes.
Glad the stacked cigarette coupons she and her husband
would buy some tool or appliance with no other way
swept down from a cluttered end table
to the oval burgundy rug—glad they remain,
everyone staring or starting to reach for the coupons
scattered the way I left them from my movement

to break away with my cousins running

to the other room, away.

JEWDOG

I turn the page with my tongue
to study an enlargement of the frog
and two small armored dogs—I study
the Fury with a tongue of nails
pressing behind them. My nose moistens
over the pet devil guarding a nun. I turn the page
to study the painted layers of a knight's armor
and the mast of a boat with a cargo of hands.
I'm licking the paint for the last time,
looking at Hieronymous Bosch for the last time,
looking at Saint Anthony and the virgin blood
in the human-sized frog's cup
for the last time. I lick the shrubs
where the dogs came through, erasing them,
erasing the painted table and the painted path,
erasing the cleaver and the bowls prepared
for the dog's meat.
I'm chewing on David Wolper's celluloid,
The plumber who puts in the gas-line
and not a water-line to the showers goes down
in the acids of my saliva, cursing Jews.
The celluloid is crackling around my eye lids.
I lick the smoldering edges off, I lick the paint
off an idiot's head, I lick the paint of the pet devil
for the last time, I erase the painted egg it produced,
I lick the closed door of the tiled room,
and the leather sweat-band of a helmet
a guard left against the door jamb-
I lick the German conductor's fingers,
they smell of dumplings and vaginal juice-
I lick the threshold of the door
where the music carries you away.

But they went off already,
the procession of Jews,
the armored dogs too
are going, the get-up they're in
won't help. I run at the legs
of a girl who is the color of ripened limes,
I do it so she'll get out of here if she doesn't know.
I'm looking at the winged executive for the last time.
I watch him land on the table where she sleeps.
I watch him and the guards preparing
the lime-colored one for the last time.
He's taking her bladder to transplant
for his pet Rottweiler—he's taking her hair
for the heads of his upholstered dolls.
His cock reaches across the room. I watch him jar
the bladder in the preserving solution,
I watch him fold the hair down for the last time.
Looking into her open skin he says, "I do not have roses,
I do not need roses, but you—you are a lime
wrapped in a rose, and you must pay
for your rose, have you forgotten?"
Nothing but hair rolled by hand
into separate stacks. Nothing but French ants,
German ants, Croatian and Ukrainian ants
carrying their packages of hair away.
Nothing but papers for transport,
nothing but contracts, little death-carts of hair,
nothing but hardware salesmen departing for the Mideast,
nothing but statistics, nothing but reports.
I'm licking her feet, I'm washing
the lime-colored one's feet,
staring down at the linoleum of Portland,
sweating into the booth, eating in there,
writing and pausing. Nothing but a Jew's dream.

Abrams

That was Abrams, the tiler from the Borscht Belt,
that deli man lifting a case of oil to the upper shelf.
Those were his forearms, his tattoo.
Abrams who I worked for after the crate-building gig.
Abrams himself who learned to set tile in one of the camps-—
does it matter which one?—and who taught me and gave me
an old trowel with a worked-in wooden handle . . .
It's the same stew and coffee after work
as it was in the morning, the same worker's newspapers
and Elizabethan plays I reread five years and fourteen years
later. Walking all over again in the neighborhood
thinking about the strikes, thinking about the lies and imbalances
left unmet and the consequences
of not knowing anything else. I walked in Abrams thinking about tile,
I carried his oil, a deli man was my teacher, he paid me for overtime,
in my body I memorized every move—I was going to impress Abrams
who wouldn't tell you if he was impressed, spoke hardly at all, only
                              about tile,
and his son who also did tile, and the other child from Chelm
pushing a wheel barrow piled with mortar, and his teacher
the German foreman, supervisor of tile-setters, singing
                              in the shower stall,
and the youngest, from Chelm, his eyes clenched, eating a salted rag
with intense pleasure and a sweating face—
a live mule he was butchering on the shower floor—
that was King Hades' cantor—the foreman singing and singing—
and whether the hide comes off clean with a good knife or not
he doesn't decide if it goes for lamp shades—or if an ear is cut away
for sausage, or for good luck, or a keepsake for an officer's whore,
or if the mule is made a converted Jew before the knife begins
so when it is killed there will be one less Jew in the world—
there's no guarding, there's no preparing, no deciding

if a tail is put aside for soup, or a whip,
or if the guts will be used to make violin strings if there is time
for violin strings before the Death Tango begins—the Lithuanian guard
hums the Death Tango to himself over the snorting muzzle
                        and the slack ears of
the mule farting blood—that is Abrams' forearm in the Death Tango,
it is a handle without a cup, that tiler with only a handle, such a thing
dancing, such a thing spreading adhesive on the wire lath
so evenly—he speaks hardly at all, only what has to do
with tile, the youngest from Chelm, his pure stroke.

Ukrainian Bird

A Ukrainian bird came to me in the carob,
muted brown with a green throat. Ukrainian
because it had the face of my mother's last uncle,
Benjamin, the skinny one, the ice-skater and seducer,
the Communist pamphleteer. He visited me from all that way,
sometimes you can, most of the others don't bother, or can't.
His face was wild, he had no hands to gesture with,
he whistled to me hopping in along the branches heavy
with brown fruit. He was trying to tell me something big,
even strategical, I couldn't make it out. Then he tried to—
but I wouldn't let him—put his head under his raised wing,
under his overcoat, to sleep again or maybe fly
back to Kiev, to his nest carpeted with documents
proving the family descended from King David, who else?
But I wouldn't let him and he was whistling again and hopping
out of control, the ice-skater's trance again,
the sound-track to stirring things up again.
After that he looked at me like he didn't know me
when I tossed him bits of hash browns
on the food-stand patio tile, when, actually
that's the way they eat on that side of the family,
so consumed
they ignore who's there.

Anna

Got onto the bus anyway when her third grandson's first daughter was born
in the worst heat in March since eighteen something—stepped in with all

eighty-four years of her folded green tickets to the morning and her packet
of red tickets to the evening almost used up—trundled and pushed herself

up three flights with her complaining about knees and joints of hot fluid,
supplications to the unattending but exasperatedly imagined grandchildren—

she was either in her forest green dress with the red and gold paisleys or the
vermillion one with the stitched on green dots under rayon silk blended

scarves with cerulean and magenta and opaque white florals, rhinestones
barnacled to her lapel and collar, cultured pearls and Woolworth

jeweled head bands and the small diamond ring no visitor to her apartment
could depart from without complimenting while she held up her hand

with a self-aware empress-like nonchalance dropped forward from her wrist
as though it was a rare exhibit, and on her hand it was a rare exhibit

because all she really knew was vanity, the charm of
transparently premeditated vanity in an old woman,

and her vanity was renowned, she held forth, you believed it, her vanity
was generous not exclusive, you understood it, you were with her swathed

in her vanity, you lived beside the folds of her big body, held up
and hidden by it in the illusion of what was ultimate in yourself—willfully,

predeterminedly, as though it was a palpable substance she secreted.

In her seventies when her daughter joked and prodded her
about her older-and-much-heavier-than-herself-who-was-huge

second husband—she let out a comical insinuating laugh pounding
the palm of her hand and chanted "like a man thirty-five, daraling,

like a man thirty-five . . ."
And that, before the fragrance past dying not yet born had begun,

and the craterous vaccinations sagged toward her thighs,
and her kelp-beds of fake jewelry were in the drawer permanently

and she cursed her God, "May he have the ears of mouse,
may he live inside my first husband's carbuncles."

But she was enchanted in front of the crib, briefly recovered from
what started absorbing and blotting-out the stems of her voice,

the lining of her heart, her ear lobe hairs, everything. And her throat
the ten-day mouth warmed, the great-grand-daughter moving there,

breathing on the fat swell of Anna's tits rising and backstreaming,
a precious pink moth of the infant hand now waking,

wavering toward Anna, holding the face in the soiled bonnet,
chewing with lip-covered teeth the fingers and the fat arm—

shaking her head and dipping it, Anna humming,
Anna's mouth holding a plump moth, raising and shaking up

the blue rattle, the orange flame of her lipstick tinting
the child's face, the wild fluid

feeding Anna's eyes.

PART TWO

Cook

I walked in by the salad station
where I could sit a few minutes
and smoke before going on.
I came back to relieve
my half brother in the middle of
a ten-hour split shift. Seeing me
by the stainless steel and the white flour,
he smiled with one cheek
and pointed to his shirt pocket,
then to his mouth,
and I gave one of the waitresses
my cigarettes for him to take from.
Sat there for a while smoking
away from the direct heat I would
be in front of soon enough.
The two guys that did preparation
went over the list with me. The one
I was training to work the broiler
kept calling me sir, and I told him
to forget that whether he was used to
talking that way or believed he had to
because he needed me to get more money.
If anything, there was no Union there,
and I should be kind so he would think
twice about it if they offered him my job
at 2/3's the pay or less. They moved on,
one to the storeroom, one to the freezer.
I stood among the stripped outer linings
of shrimp and quartered hunks of chicken,
my neck bones bobbing in their own sauce.

I brought out my knives and my apron.
The meat was waiting. I needed the job.
I moved down to the larger cutting board
with a pair of bloodied hands
and the desire to take nothing.

CLINIC

All I know is the one day I didn't
walk my daughter into the Dental Clinic
I saw a van with stolen license plates
pull from the alley, a van
with curtained windows driving
up to the side entrance. One time,
you know, and I see the cellar
with bones and small skirts.
Pulling away alone I see
Salvadoran skeletons
from the news photo,
mostly children's bones
piled in a ditch by mutilators
trained at Fort Benning, Georgia.
I see mockingbirds chewing black hair.
And I see the squat oaf
who dismembered a boy
in a wooded golf course area
north of here a month ago—
I see the bailiffs and the guards, the lawyers, the judge
and the newspaper-television-entertainment-goons
trying to interview the mother whose pitiful cunt
he pushed from and screamed and sang from
like the rest. One time—and I can't distinguish
whether a van is dropping off ex-rays
or cruising for a girl alone—to the point now
sometimes I can't distinguish when I hear certain cries
in the other apartment or hotel room
whether it is fucking I hear above me or someone
under someone who has been cruising around
in a curtained van someone else
saw pulling away.
You know what I mean.

Rye Seed

My great uncle took a pouch of rye seeds with him
from his village outside Kiev
and gave me one 34 years later in Los Angeles
when I was five. A rye seed from 1921 or 22.
He met Chagall in Paris . . . a few words at an exhibit . . . he was 19.
He was part of the exiled Jewish Communist circle that didn't fight
in the revolution. He was a Tolstoyan vegetarian and wore shoes
      made of rope. In Baltimore, then later in Detroit, he made it
photographing children on a pony before he got fed-up with being a tailor,
before the chicken-ranch years in Petaluma
that saved him. I know maybe 2, 3 like him—that gentleness that never
made a child feel slow. I see him, the way he handled his little black jewels
in the linen seed bag, convincing the five year old of the worth
beyond their size, and how he saved that one for him alone
for that day he met him. He always sided
with working people when the family argued about strikes.
He lied about the psychopath Stalin to the family and to himself
until it was okay not to. I have no idea how the lies haunted him
after losing a sister and four cousins in the Russian concentration camps.
He gave me a rye seed and my father put it in a shot glass on the table
next to my bed when he put me to sleep. I don't remember
when I lost track of it, that sliver of a coal left unburnt in memory.
I see every leaf of the ashes that are now its only cup.
Not exactly my favorite ashes.

GREGOR SAMSA'S FACE

Nabokov, who went so far as to make
diagrams of the fictional apartment
Gregor Samsa lived in as an insect,
did not talk once about
Gregor Samsa's face.
Why he didn't, I don't know.
It couldn't have been a pleasant face—
that insectization of a man's lips, for instance.
And we too would turn away
from that mouth the way we turn
from the dog's lick
after yelling at him
for eating shit.

And there is something
of a man being
only worthy of shit
in Gregor Samsa's
being turned into
an insect who
eats garbage
however considerately
it is served up.
And I used to see
the same world
in the rundown apartments
where I worked as a carpenter.
I saw it
in the way the tenants
offered me drinks
in glasses not unclean
but smeared from
so much ground

into them—glasses
they couldn't replace—
drinks they really couldn't
afford to offer.
And driving back
from those apartments
I saw it on the bluff
above Route 1
where the insect-people
had come from the colder
cities to live
in the open. . .

I come to Gregor Samsa's face
and to the frozen face
I saw once
in a subway dwelling,
a face with hard
red hair,
like Van Gogh's face,
an injured saint
or fool that all
brothers are
who have beards
like the beard I imagine
on Kafka's character,
and who don't know how
to stop themselves
from getting swindled.

But as for Gregor Samsa:
a man's beard
caught on fire,
and three others came
to warm themselves.

HAD TO BE

Had to be those two punks tormenting a pigeon
in Portland. Had something wrong with its wing,

raising it up crookedly to thrash back at them. Had to be

wasted to some little shit thing to hound a pigeon
broken under a bench. And they liked it, pitching
rolled-up bags of garbage at that mess of a bird.

I told them they ought to stop, and L hated that I did this,
didn't have sympathy for those two petty sadists, but didn't
want me challenging them either. The one wearing a clear

green plastic cross said, "you can stuff it man." And I told L
to wait a minute and stepped between them and the pigeon.
Then the sneering started and they backed away
telling me to "fuck-off," and one of them reached

for his inside coat pocket like he had something, but he
didn't have anything. And walking out of the park they turned
yelling something else, giving me the finger. L tried to lift the bird out

from under the bench, but it pecked her hand viciously,
breaking the skin on her knuckles. I wrapped a handkerchief
on my fingers while she went to the fountain

to wash, but the pigeon pecked and flapped skirting farther
under the bench into some bushes when I reached for it. Then L,
patting her hand, leaned down to where I was and said, "let's just go."

Two Puppets In One

I never wanted a watered-down story
and I still don't. Every denial leads to lobotomy,
everything watered-down is a pack of lies.
The worst lie is the way they've set up and advertised
the scarcity of work—so every puppet in the audience
is grateful to have any available job in the system:
paint-scraping puppets, pipe-fitter puppets, part-time
toxic clean-up crew puppets, factories of women puppets
packed and bunched at counters because they can fit more
of their smaller bodies into the factory space—a puppet majority
fits right in.

When I started out, when I was nineteen,
back when I was on delivery at *Soul Charm BarBQ,*
when I was a hopeful puppet, maybe only
a quarter of a puppet, after my car exploded and I became
the dishwasher, back in the middle of that winter
when the night cook flipped out on *black beauties*
and stabbed himself in the thigh—they didn't have a choice
and yanked me over from the sink—that's how
I started in the kitchens. Worked mostly on the broiler mostly
for a lot of bad owners. No one, no one, I'm one
of the last puppets who will say it: all smiling workers are liars,
and the one ass-wipe Rabelais didn't mention is in the velour
of hating bosses—which must explain why
—in the powerless logic of being a puppet hating bosses—
during the years 1971-1983 I lived
in an apartment with bathroom so small
you had to shit sideways.

FLOATING FORESTS

If I knew what to feed the field-bugs
who missed the way back underground
and came to warm themselves under my lamp

I would get it for them. They don't
touch my parsley, they don't come near
my sour dough roll . . . I was looking out at
the floating forests called the Salt Spring Islands.
I was finishing the poem that would be called
"Introduction to My Face." I didn't know

what to make of the Navaho story-teller,
I didn't know if I could make the connection,
or if it mattered to either of us. For me,
it's impossible the way they wait for winter

when bears and what they represent
and spiders and what they represent
have gone underground before
they begin their story-telling
ceremony. I would miss what
the spiders and bears take with them,

I would miss the ice and the dirt
that sticks to their fur, I would miss
everything the ethnologist in the footnote
calls their negative potentialities. . .

A uniformed man with a face that was
all fangs and saliva was the last thing
I saw before waking. I would feed him
too, but he went back under.

As it is I am in Solon
where I contain a leg-brace.
I put my leg up on the booth,
I alternate which leg to put where.
I don't know if the girl with a leg-brace

understands a language to complain in
or if an unanswerable speech has strained
her mouth at the corners like that. I don't know
why the floating forests are so impenetrable,
why the fangs and saliva surface and go back
under, why the spiders, why the bears—

I don't understand the ritual of
the Navaho story-tellers, I don't understand
the conditions of their Muse, or if I am supposed to,
or if it matters.

I'm looking out of the video-store-hardware-pharmacy-
pre school-retirement center-gas station-market from
the diner side window. The smoke in here is part of the furniture.
I don't know how to express this pock-mark
of a street, in Solon, at 4 o'clock in the afternoon.
I don't know the right way to look at the naked part

of her leg where the brace had been
loosened. I don't know how to take in
the involuntary ugliness of the big shoe
kicked a little to the side.
Watching her reposition the brace alone,
I adjust in my own booth her weight
on the back of my throat. . .

I was looking out at the floating plums
above the puddled ground.
I am the leafy part
of the unclear water,
I am the worn through part.
I am looking down into it again,
looking down from the shed I was building,
looking at the garden flooded here and there
with rain, looking into the cloth with legs
and plums leaking from it.
I am part of the over-ripeness
of plums fallen, broken-apart flesh,
the skin curled down through sparse grass,
I am part of the unstable shadows, plums of water
beside them.

Rattled

What I'm about
is a rattle, the kind
you can see the wood grain
showing in the stem,
not one with a slick painted handle.
Mine's that used one.
I was never about a rattle so fine
it is kept in a case or the back of a drawer
for some marked occasion. And I need it.

Right now, some way I
don't know from before I don't know
where I am, and I need that rattle
with the worn down stem,

I need to shake up
the flying embryo broken off
inside of it. Not just any rattle will do.

The Style of My Vengeance

My vengeance was to pull one thread
and have all the patches
fall off.

My vengeance was the blind one
blaming the ditch.

There were too many extremes within me:
my vengeance was pissing on the tree
of my mind.

In his robe with one arm torn away my vengeance sat
picking at a comb with broken teeth
leaning forward telling me,
"I landed you the graveyard shift
at Bilair Pillow factory."

And all the time it was my vengeance
leading the ants I could never get rid of,
the ants I finally had someone come out
and spray chemicals for.
It was that kind of enigma
like Osiris buried with a hard-on,
like my vengeance *was* Osiris,
my fertility nightmare.

My vengeance was the mechanic
finding the smell
had been a rat
dead inside the dashboard.
For days I hadn't said a thing.
How sly I was, how sly
my vengeance let me be.

My vengeance was the giant
unbalanced figure
lethargical and strategical
as myself.

My vengeance was the knife
that could whittle its own handle.

My vengeance had a monkey's
face and a horse's ass.

My vengeance said,
"If a man is destined to drown
he will drown
in a spoon full of water."

My vengeance, how little
I expected you.

PART THREE

MY PICO BOULEVARD

I'm back on Pico Blvd again,
my 1954 again.
I'm staying beside the fat tailor on Pico,
staying with the mice he fed,
and I'm looking at his hands
he smoked yellow
in here
in a tailor shop
so small and usually empty
I sometimes didn't notice it
from the moving streetcar.
He fed himself to the pins
in here.
I'm staying with the Casals of Pico.
He used to hunch down in front of
the half-empty hangers swaying
over the neck of his sewing machine,
music or no music,
hunched down, hairless
not in a black shroud,

I remember, like Casals—
so tasteless for a man who worked with cloth
to be untailored like that.
Not a black shroud
but a left-behind black wool blend
he cleaned and repaired,
unpaid for,
sometimes hung up out of the way
so as not to get soiled with smoke
while he worked and swayed
hunched this way and that way.

Eleven years later I watched
the good Isaac Stern,
all that glamour, and all the shops artificially
thriving on Wilshire. The leases there
too steep for Casals of Pico
nine years after
or before his death.

Isaac Stem and The Queen of American Wheat
celebrating on Public Television.
The Emperors of GM and U.S. Plastic
were in the box across from her:
the glamour, the service, the control
that never weakens.
And Casals of Catalan
hunched-down as though under the butt
of a Falangist rifle . . . it was a celebration
of the Wilshire Boulevards of Madrid
and Los Angeles, not the Picos,
not even Casal's birthday—
that one last piece stroked out
at ninety through the closing orifice
of his music. And the two violinists
were pure Pico the way they got him,
Casals, when it was over.
And the way they threw themselves toward
the hunched figure not seeing
how Wheat and Plastic were making them
accomplices to their loyalties—not seeing
the way it was confused with every disadvantage.

And the way they seemed to be carrying him
or holding onto him floating under
their hands back to his seat

where Casals sank beside his wife
into his cape. . .

And I'd like to be soothed
by him too, genius of the Old Beauty:
Bach, Mozart.
But I'm looking at what I've got,
at this 1994 Pico
and at the woman springing out
from the car door and then screaming back
into the closed window, "Bitch! I'be back
f'you bitch!" That Pico,
that bestial mouth eating
from Mozart's ear,
eating from the driver's thorax,
eating from the passenger's window.

That Pico,
where the road cuts over from Highland
further down to eat LaBrea
with its beaten storefronts
and apartments, identical
storefronts and apartments
intimate with the Casals of Pico.

I get off the bus at the Rimpau Terminal
with Shogun, Iron Maiden, and El Stranger,
all of them reeking
of beer and lighter fluid
and no idea Casals
was ninety the night before,
and no idea
what the people who make the stuff they're stoned on

make or don't make on them.
I get off at the Rimpau Terminal
in the skin of a young man
who dreams he enters a street car
to leave this world—

and to have had the dream before,
but to have entered
the hog of Pico
not the Blue Car to Ocean Park.
Then eating my way back through the snout
to get out of Rimpau,
to re-enter my squat tailor's world,
my 1954 again, planted beside
the black cigarette burn marks
in the maple counter,
below the smoke full of whips
my tremendously fat grandfather exhales
with his chest like a street car booth,
with his completely slow body and miserable dignity
of making it and not making it
as a tailor for 55 years.

And I reek of rye bread again,
my thumb reeks of butter.
I reek of the rubber street car floor
where I sat and ate my corn meal crust
to hold me over until dinner.
I reek of spools of thread and the cost of cloth,
I reek of a harvest of dull buttons,
gabardine paid for on credit,
wool stacks weighing their branches
to the concrete slab,
the smaller branches at rest on my back
in a rough bloom of thread

in a coat he stitched together
and pressed with his hands reeking
of cleaning chemicals and smoke. . .

I'm walking with Señor Brass Balls and El Ninja
looking down from the Food Value market wall,
I'm walking with my own graffiti,
my own Ivan Yakovlevich who cut open a fresh roll
in the morning and found a human nose.
And me: finding only the bus at Pico
where I'm coming out the door with a short paycheck
because I wouldn't work sick.
I'm walking with Yardstick
El Samurai, Shaggie and Ivan—
going to the Gas Company office
where I pay half,
then to the Edison Co. office
because I owe them from last month.

Getting off the bus
in the neighborhoods around Pico and Crenshaw,
around LaBrea, around Redondo Boulevard
where you get so stuck in it you have no idea
what Wheat does to Crenshaw
or what Plastic does to Pico—
you have no idea
there are such Emperors—
and you go back and forth on a bus
about which if they were to comment
they would say
they are neither glad
nor otherwise to know
it exists.

HER FRIDAY

Ron Aslavsky's mother used to
come back in the summer months
with sweat rings completely down
her sides from pressing clothes
all day at Midtown Cleaners.
That Friday I slept there
she came back with eyes that ate
from a bare hill, but her mouth
wasn't some withered plum,
it was moist and full of hot color.
She was tired and cooked what she had
for us, and she wasn't conciliatory
about it. She was going out after her bath
and we could watch any movie
or play cards, whatever we liked.
It was before it was ripe enough
for the man to pick her up
and to meet her son. She knew how
to keep outside from either of those two
and I can tell you she wasn't going out
with some guy who had only part of a nose:
there was none of that fungus
of not being touched about her at all.
And when Aslavsky looked up like he needed
to be told to wipe his face
she ignored the gesture
and asked if he wanted more.
"Dontcha want more honey?"
I can hear her asking from that delicatessen
she now serves in underground. Back then
she'd pile up the food and bring it into
the part of the kitchen where

the table was built-in and
I wanted to be inside of
ever since I saw her
through the bathroom window
shaving under her arms.
And we ate all the stuff she slid
onto our plates—onions, potatoes, salami
she scrambled into half a dozen eggs
lasting inside of us for hours.
I liked her, I liked her for it all.

Chaos With Waterfowl

Another man's woman in a dream, lifting her up,
paneled room darkening, held her standing
against a wall . . . when your face appeared.
An underground room
bordered you, a room
with a vine-covered piano,
boxes of paints, ragged shoes,
white-washed canvases
stacked or leaning
against walls. . .
unfinished dolls. . .
hardened clay...
sweaters and newspapers
piled on chairs.
Dragging parts of myself
into that room
in my rotten cloth,
that clothing underneath
my nakedness
I had only begun
to see through.
I thought I came to lie
by the window where you had
called me over to see
a waterfowl, a sanderling
briefly out of place there
poking among the piled
lemon blossoms.
I thought I came to stay
by the window or rake blossoms
with you who stared
from an underground room

in a rude dream.
I didn't see yet the dead end
at the table with its few
camellias floating
on the water
in a cut
glass bowl. . .
I wasn't floating,

I was looking
through cut shapes
that covered the table.
And it seemed comforting
in the middle of
my chaos the way
the simple cloth
lapped over
and brushed
my knees
when I drew
under it,
and then began to
portion food in pieces
for our two girls
from separate families.
I didn't see how
out of it I was.
"How 'bout that,"
 I said looking out
at the sanderling,
a dirty scavenging
bird, really,
who was lost for awhile,
cleaning itself within

a pool that formed
in the broken part
of the pavement,
then made its quick ascension
soaked with droplets.
But I couldn't see
that waterfowl clearly
if it was perched on my hand.
And you were part of that too,
you put together something
for yourself out of
that chaos of mine.
And how were you
supposed to stop it?
—that fumbling
keeping me blind and out of
which you gained
a kind of power.

Marc Chagall and the Male Soul

I don't know if
the peak of the male soul is carried
with a woman above towns and orchards.

I'm not sure if it isn't the reverse
that is true, or at least
also true to the same woman

descending—entering through her door
of painful blood
her door of low wages and insomnia—
entering only to be
consoling not flying
at all.

And perhaps Chagall had bypassed
or outlived and was not concerned
with painting those moments.
But what do I know of Chagall
with his floral ejections!
His wife on a green donkey
or a horse of purple blood.
What do I know of
the animals and the botany
of Chagall—aviator of red gardens!
What do I know?
The male soul has mostly seemed
like something I could
not grasp, something fictional,
something with roots in a mirror
beyond what I can perceive,
or that's how I conveniently perceived it

and he is the one
I could never empty my pockets for
but kept in my pocket
as a keepsake—even while
mounting the sweating horse
of purple blood,
maybe even while
consoling a woman.
That male soul too
with its ragged attachment
to being dispensable.
I'm looking at that,
looking at it possibly too late,
I know, and I know I have chosen
that too, even methodically
in some way.

SOME 1948

A little bankruptcy and mercy mixed into it all for me,
and bankruptcy and bloody corns and pre-natal depressionisms.
Everything my mother recalled: her Fan Tan gum, her Chesterfield Kings,
and pressing clothes till eleven at night most of nineteen months
in her younger sister's shoes, my father soaking up to his knees
in the flooded basement of their cleaning business, going broke,
rats scuttling out of the reach of his raised galvanized pipe.
"And, can you believe it?" she says, "a puny one
kept staring right at him chewing a sock he left on the handrail."
At my conception my father says, "Aren't you going to douche?"
"No." And he falls off into sleep mumbling, "You're crazy. . . shake'a1eg. . .
who cares?. . . tootsy frootsy." What a conception the combined act
of mercy and bankruptcy and a little passion is. Bankruptcy and mercy
my "more" and my "not enough" are born in, literally. Bankruptcy and mercy
has its own gullet that got me here, which reminds me,
I shouldn't forget I've always been eluding getting scorched
in mustard douche in one form or another
or did the robot I've been 1/3 of my life convince me
it was that way? I'll be looking at that until the end. Just a little passion
after fixing the pipes. My parents in their early 30's, a watery blue tone
goes with the memory, really it's more an indigo rhododendron
petal tint surrounding those two I leaked from, just enough.
But they don't flare in their blue so much, they don't have
the incandescence as much as Chagall's watery blue.
It isn't the same. At my conception it's the end of 1948,
and Chagall's kind of blue
was drained out of the species by then.

Driving Face Down

Now I see myself in that banged-up truck—the dents
in the tail-gate and fenders were the sepals and spathe
I burrowed and sank within. In my work as a carpenter
I beat in the body of that truck, always lugging
too much, always sawing lumber on the hood
or tail-gate pulled-down, too tired to set-up sawhorses
too rushed, too packed with materials, too broke

to care. Now I see how—next door to a place I remodeled—
I side-swiped that car, of all cars a '61 T-Bird then in '86
already a classic—everyday I passed an older saw-faced man
and his two beer-drinking sons working it into cherry condition—
quiet gruff types, always drinking—other cars
all over the lawn and driveway. And I felt like they wanted
to beat me for tearing back that bumper, not bother
to have me replace it all, not bother them to breathe again
or pay for any of it. . .

these sons were controlling something
they hadn't controlled sometime before
and they paid for it—I could tell by the way
the father did most of the talking, backing
them out of the way from where
they leaned at me out of their tools
and grease, fire of blow-torch
and soldering-gun . . . he spoke of the cost and rarity
of what I damaged, telling his boys to go back
to changing hoses and tightening valves
and that he would "take care of it . . ."

I went with him to some specialty parts place
and found the same—what he insisted was the same—
expensive bumper, paid for it and it was done . . .
they were one of those hells you earn
by your own sloppiness and negligence
because it wasn't an accident— I hit that car
and dug them up . . . I was driving face down
burrowing into something too dark in myself
to see out from when I hooked that bumper—
I was face down listening to Rebetika-music,
songs of those Greeks damned and assimilated
in Turkey, songs of the barren kettle,
wandering, and the worst kinds of labor . . .

But that whole time I was hearing the music
of no songs and no boundary, songs that dug holes
and walked me into them—fermenting deeper—even
at the bottom of the music I was driving from,
within dented doors and fenders—my sepals and spathe,
my mess—descending a hill in Los Angeles fumes,
my family broken, eating it face down, unperceived,
driving, not seeing, nothing to mollify the damage
of what had burnt-up, just some carpenter driving
among pouches swollen with nails, bevel square, wood
and drywall dust, lumber materials 'blunt dirty edges—
all to go entering rooms that were going
to be pulled down and reshaped—and my partner's
loud rock-music songs with their obsession
with being touched—yelling down with it, to have it,
to be continuously reminded of it . . . and then to me

sounding of the wretchedness you cannot sleep through,
eat or work through . . . to me tasting the sweat of the journey
up the driveway, the little dance, the scuff-walk

that was done to dilute humiliation of ripping a stranger's car
because I didn't look—and yelled down my mournful music,
and they heard it, and came out to stand around
in the hell of the explanation I made to them
outside their den of ratchets and blow-torch fire.

MASK

It's not much better
in the room containing masks.
You have to know them:
the iridescent feathers,
the intense labial shells—
not only the dominance
of the lower side, the least
competence, the least excess,
not only the husks or the animal teeth
that also order you around
to serve them. You have to know
masks, and you have to know
when the betrayal is coming,
or is it insight you think you
don't want until you see
the mask below the face,
what doesn't come raised
in recognizable features, acceptable
expressions? You have to be able to read
that too, read how you speak and what
you speak through it. You have to know.
But what does it do? I think you have to
part away the wood of masks completely,
especially the kind that opens
into another mask: the feathered faces
risen from underneath: story teller's masks.
Feathered. Shell-strung. Others with cheeks
covered up by splayed lower teeth. Absurd
because we don't live with or really care about
animals or the sea, and the hermits inside their shells
don't need us at all. I live without celebrating the old
masks, the story teller's masks, I stand against them,

all masks, really. I think the inward face
isn't enough, or the mask that refers to it.
I want to talk at the instant of the impulse
to attach them, that's all, that's
enough, for now.

And I catch myself in that room
not looking at them, but only
at the fir wood of
the stand they rest on,
the vertical grain
alert in my mind.
It's dangerous to celebrate masks
too much. And it's not important
that we tend almost with nothing
wood or images
that don't stay long.
You have to know about masks,
then you have to get out quick
and not pay too much attention to them.
Otherwise, you may find it tolerant
to be meek.

THE RED FAN

I hold up what's left of a red fan
that burned apart inside of me—I'm picking through
and discarding what remains from
my deterministic side, my lethargic side. . .
I used to tear out walls and floors. . .
I hold up what's left . . . I used to
haul things for money . . . I'm thinking
of that time I did demolition work
and how I used to take my tools off to the side
away from the crew, thinking I was clearing away
something within myself, and justified the work.
I'm admiring what survived from the red spines,
what's left inside the bowed span.
I'm watching an anxious fat crow hop around
spitting black juice, keeping us on the move—
we lifted out rafters, the teeth of roofs
we tore out walls and floors. . .
in the 70's, when I had further to roam
or hadn't drawn enough
from the end I came to,
too dumb to know what was the end
or enough . . . I'm standing with the crew
looking with shop lights under the hood
of one of their trucks—no one can figure out
what it is, we complain about the light,
we want ice on our necks and shoulders,
we want to decide and look at it tomorrow—
one of the crew walks off with me alone to brag
about a teenage whore he screwed backwards
over a table the night before, and told her
to whisper his name, and she did . . . it was always
something to be carted away—stucco and lath,

the owner of black juice, the pathetic esteem
of our names on patches or in a runaway's mouth.
But I couldn't say it then . . . a demolition man,
I was thinking of that time I did demolition work
before I could see what was left of a red fan
that burned apart in me,
before that life consumed me
and went past me, a dangerous bristle
beating the ground behind me.
I couldn't say a thing
because I didn't get it
and I was dry, too dry, and closed off
and couldn't say patiently
how any of us fit. I hold up
what's left of a red fan the mother
of demolition and diamond blades,
the mother of cocoons and caved-in stucco,
the mother of sirens and mosquitoes, sledge hammers
and shovels, the mother of stained plaster and wild petals
planted in me—it never enchanted me much—
I held it so few times—
it is the emblem of the life
I used to abandon to live—suspiciously
I dredge myself with it now, a little.

BENEATH THE JEWISH MUSIC

It took twenty-five years
to dance alone in this basement room
to an unseen clarinet and to become a plangent thread
in the oscillating wind
of my desk fan—it takes twenty-five years
to dance a stone to pieces. Twenty-five years

to reach ecstasy, not three years or fourteen years
like I bet everything on before. I thought I would dry up
from the lack of it, I thought I would always
live in the rooms beneath the Jewish Music,
rooms I abandoned,
rooms I was forced out of,
rooms for which I owed. . .

but the gardens outside—
I would like to dwell a little
on the pale mortar of the walls
and the violet bougainvillea
worn slump-stone
bordered—and on my intimacy
with the intense orange
nasturtium flower shaken
by a hummingbird that I saw
from my mattress on the floor
the first time I heard Klezmer music—and that
same day, listening to Naftouli Brandwine's clarinet—
then coming out on the porch afterwards
and sitting utterly still while the small

white-winged butterflies
mated in August in the garden

on 9th street, some of them spiraling
and linking fifty feet up in the air
above the date palms, yellow and white pallor
linking and trembling on each other's wings. . .
That's what the lucidity of ecstasy gets for you—
part of it linking and trembling, the dune of gold
                                bottle-brush pollen
piling up at the lower step, this fluttering,
this imperceptible panting. . .

Working to the Klezmer music
I thought I was a torrid bloom,
but I was only in the ninth year
toward ecstasy, I didn't know yet
how many times I would come to contradict
myself—it was the seventeenth year—no—the sixteenth—
I was always such a vague man—I was beneath the music,
and I didn't know I would end up working in a pantry kitchen
where they would call me Onion Man
because of the way I tied two damp towels—
one over my forehead low on my brows
and the other under my eyes forming a slit
I could see through just enough
while side-scraping the cut chunks
of onion under another wet towel
so the fumes wouldn't burn—I didn't know
I would discover purple onions in the pantry room
and eat them plain when they were sweet enough

or with just a heel of bread as I remembered
my great aunt telling of the delicacy
of yellow onions on hard rolls, and of garlic
rubbed on bread-heels with butter and salt
that were eaten in the winter
her sewing machine froze in Brooklyn. . .

Until maybe a few years ago I was beneath
the Jewish Music—I was only three or four years
into it when I was stunned by the rim of orange dye
shaken by a hummingbird—I had only just begun
to pull back the rock from the hole, pull
the purple onion
out of the ground
of ecstasy
when I worked in the pantry
of The Black Rabbit Inn—
I had barely entered the surging I do now
when I hear the clarinets trembling
on the violins fifty feet up in the air—
the surging and parting of myself,
the opening so far,
an Onion Man unraveling,
the being stunned by it,
what I burn, what I sweeten,
the surging out of the onion
I contain and cut open,
the one thing I grow
coming out of its tight slick vest,
out of the peels and drops
of garnet waved within
its burgundy stained coils—
wild radiance I swayed
and sang to
beside a radio this morning again
alone in a loud room to myself.